Welcome to my mind, my characters, my heartache, my pain, my love, my porn…as you embrace yourself with my stories and poems…

I'm awake now and always working

ISBN 978-0692860878

This Book Is Dedicated To

My children Christopher, Dacia, Jada, and William for always motivating me, and putting up with my "crazy," and "Him" for coming into my life
To Love and Inspire me.

My parents Marvin and Cassandra
Thanks for loving me unconditionally.

Ebony Dunson
&
Beatrice Kellum

My sisters that never stopped believing in me, and that one phone conversation that said it all!
Love you both dearly
The wait is over!

My other siblings: Chrishawna (silly one), Jermaine (twin/best friend), Christian (new hanging buddy), and Brian (calm one) y'all are some of the best siblings. My BF Jackie you are the definition of a real friend.
Love y'all always.

Thank You God
Your love is unconditional

Welcome

I never wanted to be anyone

else

I was too much in love with

the

Characters in my head

Who Could I Be

It's ironic how we met I never would have thought

but the fixation was all a coincidence your affection

and warm touch was always enough and when we

make love breathtaking it would be I never thought

one such as you could make me feel the way you do

the desire to want more was not very elusive your

fragrant I can still smell your hospitality I can still feel

this is not an illusion to me your eyes your lips

your hair I can still see but it's illogical to me

this forbidden love we're both the same leaves me to wonder

who could I be?

Sins Of A Woman

Fantasy Cum True

Some things in life we search forever to try to find the reason

But some things will remain inconclusive.

I've always been smart, independent and like things to be done my way. I'm a Legal Secretary at Smith and Smith Law Firm, I've been working here for a year and five months, the pay is great and about two months ago I started dating and sleeping with one of the brothers, thirty-five year old and sexy William Smith, which I now regret because he proved to be just like every other man I've dated not worth shit.

The only difference is William has a little more money than most men I've dated maybe that's why he cant help from being a male slut. He knows he is the total package and any woman in her right mind would love to have him, I'm just hoping for better.

We were supposed to go out after work for drinks cause William had some other engagement later. This was starting to become a pattern for him, but it didn't matter because I was starting to get annoyed with the same old bullshit. I mainly try to keep my cool for the simple reason I need my job, even though he said this relationship would not have an affect on it, but like I said I'm getting tired of the whole situation. I'm really getting frustrated with men.

"Hello Smith And Smith, LaRae speaking how can I help you," I asked as I answered the phone. "Hi this is Monica Wells calling again." This was Monica's third time calling this week she's been leaving messages for William's brother thirty-eight year old Leon Smith, but for some reason he's been avoiding her, telling me to say he's in a meeting or at court and to take a message. "Sorry Ms. Wells, Mr. Smith is still unavailable may I..." and before I could finish Monica had got very irate. "I know that fucking bastard is there, let him know if he doesn't want to talk to me over the phone, I'll just have to make other arrangements for us to meet." Trying to remain professional I replied "Okay Ms. Wells I'll give him the message," I said very dignified. I can honestly say this job has taught me a lot about professionalism, because the old me would have popped off.

After I hung up the phone I started thinking, what in the hell did Leon get himself into, and what did she mean she'd make arrangements for them to meet? Does he even know this woman? This is going to be interesting I thought. I didn't tell Leon about the call. I didn't want to give his heartless ass the pleasure of knowing what was coming, I say heartless cause at times I think he's worst than his bother when it comes to women.

It was 5:30 in the afternoon, and William and I were headed to the bar across the street for drinks. I ordered something to eat and a beer; he ordered his usual Remy and coke. We talked for about a half hour before he looked at his watch, "Baby I'm sorry I have to get going, I'll see you tonight." "Whatever," I said, with an attitude. "You know if I don't keep making money we can't keep eating," William said as he got up from the table. I knew William could care less he looked at me and left. It was cool cause I had already called an ex boyfriend of mine to come over around nine, so if William did decide to call or come over he wouldn't be getting an answer. I stayed to finish my food and my second beer I ordered.

I went home took a shower, and put on my sexy black see-through gown that I had bought two days ago. I bought it with William in mind, but since he was making some other woman happy I decided to wear it tonight. There was a knock at the door, I looked at the clock it was 9:15. I thought, this better be James. I really wasn't feeling him anymore, it's been almost a year since we broke up, but nights were starting to get lonely, and James was the only man I knew who could satisfy me. He was very long and thick, enough said.

I looked out the peephole and it was he. I opened the door and gave him a big hug. "Hi baby I missed you," I said with a smile, but it was more of what was hanging between his legs that I missed the most. James had a seat on the couch. I poured him and myself a glass of wine I had chilled on the table. "What have you been doing this past year," James asked as he took a sip of his wine. "I'm still working at the law firm, doing really good for myself, no complaints there. I just wish my love life could be better."

"What seems to be the problem," he asked as if he were really concerned. I answered with a little bit of an attitude. "It seems that every man that I've been dating is still full of play, and trying to keep a fuck orchestra, just like you were when we were together." "Girl you are crazy," James said laughing...what's a fuck orchestra?" "It's a group of impetuous women thinking they're the only one, but not knowing her guy is fucking the entire band."

"Some guys are just scared of commitment and falling in love," he said. "Well I will be glad when the scared ones turn into real men."

After talking a little more we decided to watch a movie, we didn't make it half way through before heading to the bedroom. James started pulling my nightgown slowly off my shoulders as he kissed my neck then devoured my right breast into his mouth. He finally worked his way down and started licking and sucking on my pussy just how I remembered. I sometimes enjoyed that more than the actual love making itself. After I came several times in his mouth from his remarkable tongue, he finally penetrated his dick inside me, it was extremely good, but I wanted him to put his face back between my legs.

He whispered passionately in my ear, "Your pussy is still wet and good like I remember." He then started fucking me firmer, and that just made my moans intensify. "Baby I'm cumming!" I said with a soft moan in my voice. I had cum twice already, but on the third time James and I climaxed together. He kissed me on my lips and softly said, "Damn baby I missed you." I said nothing just closed my eyes and went to sleep.

That night I had a dream that I was being made love to, and my lips below being devoured in ways I never imagined, that I couldn't keep my composure. I thought who could this be that's making me feel so exhilarating. Hell it was better than James. Whoever this person was had me so wet it was running down my ass, and then there was a whisper "*how does it feel to be with a woman?*"

The alarm clock starting beeping, and my dream came to an end; I had forgot to turn it off, it was set for my morning run, that I knew I would not be doing since James was here. It was Saturday morning, and James had left around 10:30 but not before he expressed how he wanted me back, and how things would be better, but I knew it was just the pussy that had him from last night.

I noticed that William never called or came over, and that was a good thing, I'm sure he stayed over some chick house. I couldn't help but to think about the dream I had, and the meaning for it. I cooked myself some breakfast, and then took a hot shower. I have a hair appointment at 1:30 this afternoon, and after that I'm meeting with my sister Jade to do some shopping then dinner.

It was 4:10p.m and I was just leaving the salon when my cell phone rang, "Hello," I answered. "What's going on beautiful?" It was William. "Hi William," I said hastily. "I was calling to see if you wanted to go out for dinner?" "Sorry William I'm having dinner with my sister." And before he could get a chance to respond I told him a lie that I forgot my charger and my phone was about to die, and I would call him later. I figured since he waited all this time to call me he didn't deserve dinner or my conversation.

It was 4:41 and I was pulling up to Jades house, she was outside talking to her boyfriend Dennis. "Hi Dennis, I said waving my hand. Are you ready Jade," I asked. I had no intentions on getting out of my car. "Yes I'm ready just have to get my purse." When Jade got in the car

I noticed she had my purse that I let her borrow months ago, guess she doesn't plan on giving it back.

"I see you're keeping Dennis around," I said. "Yes, He is everything I need and want, I have no complaints," she said smiling. She was happy and that was all that mattered. We made it to the mall at 5:30; we went into just about every store. Jade talked about how happy she was with Dennis, and how she sees a great future with him. I told her I'm happy if she's happy.

It was 9:00p.m and the mall was closing, we decided to go the Sports Bar across from the mall to get something to eat, and have drinks. We sat down near the pool tables so we could watch the guys play. After the waitress took our order I decided to tell Jade about my dream. I knew it wouldn't be incomprehensible to her for she had actually had an experience with a woman before. "Not you!" she said in shock.

"What do you mean not me," I asked her. "Well you have always been strictly about the dick, and I can recall the times I used to tell you about my encounters with women, and you would be so disgusted, so its very surprising to me, maybe your dream is telling you it's time to explore new things." I started thinking about how much I loved getting head. "Yea maybe," I said. After dinner I dropped Jade off back at home, and told her I'd see her later. For the next two nights I had the same recurring dream, my pussy being passionately devoured, and each time I would wake wetter than before.

It was Tuesday morning and I was sitting at my desk in a daze when William walked by. We haven't really talked since Saturday I guess he finally got the hint that I'm tired of his bullshit. It was around 10:00a.m when some woman walked into the office. She looked exotic and very exquisite. Her body was perfect, fare skin, and medium length silky straight black hair. Now don't get me wrong although I've never been with a woman I had no problem with giving compliments where due.

"Hi, can I help you," I asked. "Yes, I'm looking for Mr. Leon Smith," She said with the sexist voice I've ever heard coming from a woman, just looking and listening to her made my panties moist. Damn I must be tripping I should not feel this way. "Your name," I asked. "My name is Monica, Monica Wells." Oh shit! I thought this is the Monica that has been calling here so many times for Leon.

Immediately I started thinking of an excuse, but before I could get anything out here came Leon walking down the hall from the restroom. When Leon looked at Monica like he wanted to sleep with her I knew he had not a clue of who she was. "Hi, have you been helped," he asked. "Yes, I'm looking for Leon Smith." "Leon Smith present," He said like he had just won a prize. "And who might you be?" "Monica Wells, Amber's girlfriend." Leon's look of happiness quickly disappeared. "Can we go somewhere and talk," Monica asked. "Sure, we can talk in my office," Leon said reluctantly.

Leon's office was behind my desk, so if they talked loud enough I was sure to hear, and they were. I had to knock on his door to let him know they were that loud. Just as I thought this conversation was more interesting than the book I was reading. Monica was a lesbian, and Leon had slept with her girlfriend Amber who is now apparently pregnant by him, which he denies. It was really getting controversial in there. Monica really wanted Leon to fess up to his responsibility because Amber had decided to go through with the pregnancy and since this had caused her and Amber to break up, she wanted Leon to be there for Amber and the baby.

After Monica finished expressing how much she loved and cared for Amber, and all the love that he caused her to lose, and Leon basically telling her how he don't give a fuck! Out the office they came. "I'll be leaving for the rest of the day, so can you please reschedule all of my remaining appointments, Thanks LaRae," Leon said as he hastily walked out the main door. Monica was right behind him trying to wipe the tears from her face. She was just about to walk out the door when she turned around. "Excuse me LaRae I left my purse in Mr. Smith's office, may I go in and get it?" "Sure", I grabbed the key out of my desk drawer and opened the door.

Don't ask why I followed her into the office its not like I thought she would steal anything. "Are you going to be okay," I asked, and before I knew it I was caressing her right cheek. What are you doing I thought to myself. "I'm sorry Ms. Wells, I feel so embarrassed I shouldn't have touched your face like that." "That's okay, the way I'm feeling I could use a little comfort, Are you a lesbian?" "No I have never been with a woman." But in my head I was thinking only if you knew I've been having dreams about being with one. Monica looked at me and smiled, she grabbed a pen and notepad paper from Leon's desk, and started writing. "Here is my number, call me and thanks for caring." The entire day all I could think about is what I did, and should I call her, and if and when I do, what I am getting myself into.

Leon took the rest of the week off, guess he needed time to figure some things out. It was now Friday and I could not wait to get home, take a hot bath and enjoy my weekend. It was Friday night and I was laying on my couch reading a book, and sipping on some nice cold Moscato. I could have gone out but I chose to stay in. I did not feel like being bothered with William or James, who both called earlier to take me out. I had finished the entire bottle of wine before falling asleep on the couch. I know right, what a great life.

That night I had the same dream only this time the woman had a familiar face, it was Monica. The ring from my phone had disturbed my dream. I thought who could this be. I looked at the time it was 11:40p.m, for some reason I thought it was much later than that. "Hey LaRae." "Hi William, what's up?" "Just wanted to know if you would like some company?" I thought after being waked from my wet filled dream I could use some real loving. "Sure William you can come over." "Cool be there in twenty."

I freshened myself up a little, popped me some popcorn, and opened another bottle of wine; I love wine. William finally arrived thirty minutes later; it was late so we went straight to bed. I tried to enjoy him, and for a moment I almost did but due to my change of feelings for him I just couldn't get that into it. It was noon the next day and I made us a late breakfast. Apparently William was really hungry because out of the eight sausages I made, his greedy ass ate five.

"So LaRae," William said while still chewing on the eggs and sausage he had just stuffed in his mouth. "Yes William," I said, with that what now look on my face. "I'm going out of town next weekend, and I thought you should come with me." "Where are you going," I asked. "Texas, I have some business to handle and thought it would be nice to have you with me." "I'll definitely think about it." In my head I already knew the answer would be no, but I thought I'd tell him later.

After breakfast we took a shower, and after William left to do whatever he do best; I laid across the bed thinking what will I do today. My sister Jade was busy with her boyfriend, and since she was my best friend as well, that really gave me nothing to do. The thought of Monica came to mind, but I wasn't sure if that's what I really wanted to do. I sat on the couch, and laid there in deep thought. "What the hell! Dammit!" I guess while thinking about Monica I dozed off. It was 6:00p.m and I had five missed calls, three from William, one from James, and one from some unknown number. I called neither back, figured the day was pretty much over so I went back to sleep.

It was now Sunday, and I promised myself I would not let this day go by without doing something. I stared at that number for at least an hour, and then finally I decided to call... "Monica speaking" the voice on the other end said softly. I paused for second before thinking about hanging up. "Hi Monica, this is LaRae from the law firm." I almost felt like a child doing something I had no business. "Hi LaRae, how are you?" "I'm okay", and before I knew it we had an entire twenty minute conversation. Monica didn't have any plans, and said we could meet up for dinner around five, so I told her sure. I got off the phone second-guessing myself, but quickly thought what the hell.

It was 4:30p.m and I was making my way out the door. The drive to the restaurant felt like the longest ride ever, my nerves were getting the best of me. I arrived at exactly 5:00p.m. I called Monica to see if she was already here, she said she was inside. Calm down is all I kept telling myself, she's just a woman, it's just dinner, but that was the point I was on a date having dinner with another woman.

I walked in, and Monica was standing there with the waitress waiting to be seated. Monica asked if I preferred a booth or table; I told her a booth would be fine. As we were walking to be seated, I couldn't help but to realize how beautiful Monica really was, now I'm not downplaying myself, but Monica was absolutely gorgeous. Who would have thought me, the one who enjoyed men would be on a date with a woman, if only they knew.

The waiter that took our order knew Monica by name, so I asked her how often does she come here. She said she usually come two to three times a week, she calls it her quiet time. We talked about our current relationships or lack there of, of course I already knew about hers. Monica asked me how does it feel being on a date with a woman, I told her it was like being out with one of my girlfriends. We were there for about an hour, and I decided it was time to leave. We both had work in the morning, so we made plans to see each other again later in the week.

I drove home thinking that wasn't so bad. I finally looked at my phone that I had on silent in my purse, and noticed that William had called me five times, and left me a voice message. I listened to the message that said "call me soon as possible." I thought what could be so important. I gave him a call before pulling up at home, and apparently he was at the restaurant as well, and saw me with Monica, and wanted to know what was I doing with her. I hung up on him; I thought do not have me thinking it's something serious just to question what I am doing. Some nerve he has, and I'm sure he was there with some woman. I was finally home, and could not wait to take a shower, get in bed, and watch TV until I fell asleep.

I finally told William I had no intentions on going out of town with him this weekend, and I'm sure he could find someone else to keep him entertained. He had an attitude but of course I could care less, him questioning me was the last straw for me. The mood at the office was tense all week between us, I was just glad I was his brother's assistant and not his.

Leon seemed to be in a better mood, and that was great. I think he finally accepted that he would be a dad soon. I wondered if William told him about seeing Monica and I at the restaurant together, not that I really cared, but I was a little curious. I was glad the day was coming to an end, so I could go home and enjoy my peace.

Well it's definitely true time sure does fly when you are having fun. It has now been three months since I have been dating Monica. She thinks we are a couple, I told her I was still dating other people, but I don't think she understood; or just didn't want to. Monica had started wanting me to devote all my time to her, and even started to show up at my home unannounced. I tried to play it cool the first couple of times, but after the third time I asked her if she could please call before coming over. I wondered if this could be the reason why Amber cheated on her, or maybe she was like because Amber cheated on her.

It was a Saturday night, and I already told Monica I had plans, and that we could probably see each other Sunday. She didn't sound too pleased, but she said okay. I had started back talking to James on a regular, and we had plans for dinner tonight, and maybe a little dancing. He was trying to get this thing right between us, and since I still cared a little, I decided to give it a try. It was around midnight when we arrived back to my place. I could hear music coming from the inside, and thought I don't remember leaving the radio or television on. When I walked inside I could not believe my eyes…

I knew I couldn't trust this crazy bitch

The signs were there but I was blind to them

Lord please see me through I promise I'll go

To church on Sunday's I know I've said it before

But this time I mean it!

To be continued…

The Passion of His Strokes

So many times and so many ways it felt so good

I grew accustomed to it

So adorable so adequate I must admit I admire it

I acknowledge it

From its affection to me being affectionate

I can't deny my ambition to want to cry

So precise though it could be deceitful

But to my flesh it's so beautiful

Its approach always amiable

Always dedicated to the case

Never insecure always intellectual

To focus on the right direction

So insatiable always pleasurable

Sometimes the man himself is like thunder and rain

but it's because of this I cant deny the passion of his

Strokes

Spontaneous Love

In The Rain

It's only been three months since West and I have been dating, but I knew from the first time I met him he would be someone I could fall deeply in love with. I had let West move in with me because his previous living arrangement wasn't going so well. I figured since we were in a relationship it wouldn't be a bad idea and so far it hasn't.

West and I make love almost every day, I say almost cause I have to minus those days out of the month that little Ms. Monthly comes. Sex with West is always great I can't complain lets just say my baby is very fulfilling.

One evening, West and I had gone out to dinner; we were on our way back home hornier than two teenagers during their first time. I had started kissing on his neck and rubbing my hands on penis while he was driving. I could feel it rising and that made me want him even more. It had started raining real heavy and that's when I thought we should do something spontaneous. I whispered in his ear while still caressing his penis, "baby lets do it in the rain."

West looked at me and gave me one of his sexy ass smiles, that's when I knew he was down for it; ten minutes later we were pulling into the park. "Is this okay," West asked. "Yes baby this will do," I said smiling. We parked the car and got out running around until we found the perfect spot. Drenched we started taking off each other clothes; we had no blankets so we laid ass naked on the grass.

West had spread my legs wide open and started licking me up and down like I was his favorite flavor ice cream; he was extremely good at it. Once he was finish I got on top of him and put his love inside me. I rode him like a champ trying to win a first place trophy. I had already come twice and knew before it was over; I would come several more times. West had flipped me on my back and then onto my stomach we did it from every angle imaginable, the rain only intensified the lovemaking.

After we were finish we laid in the rain a few minutes more, we finally gathered our clothes and headed back to the car. I grabbed our jackets from the backseat, so we could put them on since that was the only piece of dry clothing we had. When we arrived home we quickly ran inside the house. We headed straight to the bedroom. I put on my meditation cd of thunder and rain. We started making love again only this time we were wet but the air was dry.

In A Daze

Her pussy still pulsating from the juices

That outflowed her body yesterday

She loved when he made her feel that way

Mesmerized in a daze as she put that moment on repeat

thinking damn she can't wait to see him again

She thought is this the shit a bitch goes crazy for

make a bitch want to kill for...Damn! All she

Could think is how she wants to be his fantasy freak

Willing to allow him to explore every part of her body

like the one no ones ever been before

Damn! Her passion runs deep like when he pulls

Her close as he enters her diamond glove and put her to sleep

Sex so powerful like her love for him consuming her mind

and soul for only him

Pussy still pulsating aching to be touched with his healing

so her walls can erupt and her river overflow

Mesmerized in a daze as she put that moment on repeat

Lust

Sinful Thoughts

It was 1:00a.m and in the solitude of their own homes they had no idea they were thinking the same thing. They were deep in sinful thoughts. She thought about calling him, but instead she put on her coat and rushed out the door. In that moment she didn't care how he would feel with her showing up uninvited. Her body needed and ached for him; she needed him and she would have him.

To his surprise there she was in the rain standing at his door in her trench coat, and red thigh high boots. He looked as if he wanted to say something as he let her in, but there was silence. She looked him in the eyes and said, "I'm sorry but I needed you." He closed the door behind her and before she could completely walk into the living space, he pushed her against the door and inserted his tongue into her mouth.

Guess he's excited to see me too, she thought. He loosened her belt tie, and as her coat fell opened, he realized she was naked. With her body still pressed to the door, he took his tongue from her mouth, "Good job," he said, and slowly started to suck on her nipples.

He pulled his penis from his pants, and then pressed his hands on her shoulders directing her to his lower head. She didn't resist and slowly went to her knees. She softly took his penis into her mouth, and begin to taste what fulfills her lower part, as she swiftly begin to move her mouth up and down, he quickly braced himself against the door, and she could feel the warm thick semen explode in her mouth. She enjoyed it and politely swallowed.

He helped her to her feet, and led her to the couch, "Take your coat off and lay down," he said. She took off her coat, and proceeded to lie on the couch. They gazed in each other's eyes for a brief second, before he stuck his tongue back into her mouth. She never use to like kissing, but for some reason she enjoyed it with him. He slowly made his way down, kissing her neck, and her breast until he finally made his way to her special spot in the middle.

Excitement went through her body as she felt the wetness of his tongue. Damn she loved when he would give her head, he would be down there for what seemed like hours. With his mouth still wet he said, "Go upstairs." His bedroom was upstairs so she knew things were about to get real. She walked into the room and laid on the bed.

He went into his closet and pulled out a bag, "look what I got." It was a brand-new vibrator; she smiled cause he listened to her about getting some sex toys so they could try new things. He opened the package and cleaned it off.

He slowly inserted the vibrator into her vagina. There was no need for lubricant, because her pussy was still wet, it stayed wet for him. As her moans grew louder so did the force of the vibrator going in and out of her pussy walls. Her legs started to shake uncontrollably, her breathing got heavier, and before he knew it she squirted everywhere! "Damn baby! I didn't know you were a squirter," he said. Funny cause she didn't know she was either. He played with her pussy for what seemed like forever to her, he enjoyed watching her squirt. As her body lay there almost lifeless weakened from all the shaking and juices that outflowed her body, he began to caress her pussy with his tongue once more. He enjoyed pleasing her.

With a hard dick he pulled her to the edge of the bed. With her legs wrapped around him he gently put it in. "Put your legs in the air," he said. As she put her legs in the air she held onto her feet, it was very pleasurable that way. After a few minutes of stroking her in that position, he told her to put her face down and ass up. As he stroked her from behind she tried to contain her moans, but it was so damn good she screamed in excitement! He didn't give a damn if his neighbors heard, to him that made him feel more of a man.

With every moan she made he fucked her even harder. In all her sinful thoughts, she thought this was the best sin she ever made. "Where you want me to put it," he asked. She opened her mouth, and once again the warm semen exploded in her mouth. She looked him in his eyes and politely swallowed.

Black Woman

You said you wanted a woman

A real black woman

To be with this real black man

But when you had me you mistreated me

Mentally and physically

From my busted lip to my swollen jaw

To my hair in your hands

To my nails broke down to my skin

That's how you treated this woman

This real black woman

Lies

Is He Or Is He Not

It was a hot summer day, and I was just leaving the restaurant with my girlfriend Trish. She's been my best friend for years. It was that day when I met him, as we approached the car, "Excuse me lady in the yellow dress," a male voice said. I knew whomever it was he was talking to me, Trish and I were the only ladies in the parking lot and besides Trish had on a red short set. At first I wasn't going to turn around, but then I thought, what the hell.

As I turned to see who this person was the first words that came to mind was damn! This dude is fine. He stood about 6'3, fare skin, nice curly hair, and deep brown eyes, he almost looked foreign, but he wasn't. "Hi my name is Eric, what's yours," he asked. "Lisa," I said with a smile. "Lisa I couldn't help but to notice how beautiful you are, and had to come introduce myself." He then proceeded to ask if I were married, single, or dating. I told him I was single, and didn't really do too much dating. He asked if we could exchange numbers because he didn't want to keep Trish and I from continuing with our plans, and that hopefully I could find some time to talk to him over the phone. I told him "sure why not."

The next day around noon Eric called me, and that's when I found out he was a single twenty-nine year old electrical engineer, no kids, had his own place, loved jazz, believed in God, and had plans to one day get married and raise a family. He asked if I had any children I told him no. I told him I had plans to have at least two when I'm married. I told him I was a photographer for ChrisDaJ magazine, and that I was taking a few business classes at the community college in Oakwood. After about an hour of conversation we made plans for our first date something simple dinner and a movie.

Eric picked me up Saturday promptly at seven o'clock in the evening like we agreed. I thought how considerate because I know how imperative time can be to me. He took me to a nice exclusive soul food restaurant with a live jazz band. Jazz while you're eating I thought how soothing and melodious. Our conversation was very consistent and cordial. We talked mostly about each other's plans for the future and our next date.

We left the restaurant around eight-thirty the movie started at nine. It was some cop movie that Eric wanted to see. I tried to keep myself awake because the movie was just that boring, after the movie we road around talking and enjoying the night air.

I finally made it home around one o'clock in the morning, of course the first thing I did was call Trish. I had to tell her how everything went. I wasn't worried about waking her she's a night owl like me. "Hello," Trish answered. "What's up Trish, its Lisa." "What's going on is something wrong," Trish asked frantically. "I'm okay, just thought I'd tell you about my date with Eric."

I told her how great the date and conversation was with the exception of the movie, and that it was a possibility he could be the one, but it would take a couple more dates to make sure. Trish told me how happy she was for me, and before I knew it my eyes were slowly closing and I was falling asleep. "Okay Trish, I'm over here half sleep, I'll catch up with you tomorrow," I said while yawning. "Okay girl talk to you later." I went to sleep thinking he's definitely the one.

After about five months of dating things where going really great between Eric and I. I was totally one hundred percent sure I was in love. Eric and I had talked about me moving out of my one bedroom apartment in the city into his three-bedroom house in the suburbs. After a few days of thinking it over I agreed. Life seemed so much better and I was a lot happier.

I was happy until about two months of us living together. I started to notice a change in Eric's attitude. He began to get aggressive and very demanding. He wanted me to cook, clean, iron his clothes, and run his errands, which wasn't a problem but he wanted it done every day. He knows I work fifty hours a week and go to school three days out the week, but none of that seemed to matter anymore.

It was a Monday afternoon and that's when the real dramatic change happened. I had just arrived home from work around five-thirty in the afternoon; Eric arrived about a half hour later. When he came in the house he went straight to the kitchen. "Where's dinner?" he yelled. I asked him why did he have to yell, and explained to him that I had just arrived home myself, and that we could order out. Eric walked over to me and gave me a look that I had never seen before; he looked as if he had seen his worst enemy, and before I knew it Smack! Right across my face, I couldn't believe the man I loved unconditionally had just hit me. "You ungrateful bitch!" he said with so much hostility… "Didn't I tell your ass I wanted my dinner prepared every day, and ready by the time I get home; now get in the kitchen and fucking cook!" It's funny cause the only thing I could say was "baby I'm sorry I'll get started right away."

The next morning at work I called Trish on her cell phone to let her know what happened. She told me to leave him cause things were only going to get worst, and that I could come and stay with her until I found my own place. Don't ask why I did not listen to her or why I stayed with Eric, maybe it's because all I kept thinking about was I love him, it only happened once and that maybe he was mad about something at work, and chose that day to take his frustration out on me. Well over the next few months that thought would serve to be not true. I did everything Eric asked, but that didn't seem to stop the mental abuse or the ass kicking I received at least once a week.

My job was on the line because I had been calling in a lot. I didn't want my co-workers to see my bruises or how much pain I would be in at times. I have fare skin so make-up really doesn't help the cover-up. Trish had stopped talking to me she said she couldn't stand to see me this way anymore. Shit! How could I blame her, I couldn't even stand it.

Sitting at home one Friday morning I had a lot of time to think while Eric was at work, I mostly thought about the shotgun that he kept in the bedroom closet, and feared that he may one day use it on me. I have seen a lot of domestic situations on the news where the outcome was not so pleasant some resulting in death. I kept thinking how I didn't want to be victim, not in my house and defiantly not on the news. It was around eight at night when Eric finally arrived home.

"Lisa baby, where are you," he called out. I was sitting on the bed when Eric walked into the room. "Hey Eric," I said softly. Eric walked over to the bed and started hugging, and kissing me, he talked about how much he loved me, and how he was so sorry for everything he had done to me. I started thinking maybe God answered my prayers. Eric had told me to close my eyes, I was a little reluctant at first for obvious reasons, but with the way he was talking and acting, I did not think that he was up to no good so I closed my eyes.

"You can open them now," he said. I opened my eyes, and in his hand was what appeared to be at least a 3-karat diamond engagement ring. "Lisa will you marry me," he asked smiling. My heart was saying yes but my mind was saying hell no! "Umm, I don't know," I said nervously. If you could have seen the look on his face when I said that, it reminded me of the way he looked the first time he ever hit me, only this time he looked much worst. "Umm, you don't know...fuck do you mean you don't know, the money I spent on this ring, and I just apologized and all you can say is you don't fucking know," he yelled!

I sat there with tears starting to roll down my face, almost frozen just waiting for him to hit me. I thought isn't life a bitch, after all the freaking abuse he had the nerve to ask me to marry him, and even worst to think that my answer was wrong. "I love you but..." and before I could finish there it was, what I was fearing would happen another ass kicking, only this time he had the nerve to force himself on me after he was done, and tell me he was sorry while screwing the hell out of me. After he was finished he rolled over and went to sleep.

I laid there for a few minutes before I went to the bathroom, my body was in so much pain it hurt to even walk, as stood looking in the mirror, All I could do was break down and cry, I looked horrible and I felt it too. I went back into the bedroom, there I stood over Eric while he slept and pulled the trigger. Yes I did it, I killed him with the gun that I feared would one day kill me. I sat there for what seemed to be forever but it was only few minutes, and then I called the police.

You would have thought when the judge seen all my bruises and heard what I went through he would have showed some mercy, maybe he did I got five years in jail and five years probation. Judge said I should've called the police instead of taking the law into my own hands. I wanted to tell him fuck you and fuck the law!

I had time to think about Eric and all the good times we shared, and how it all came to this. How in my heart I still loved and missed him. It's a fact there is no certain time limit for a person to reveal their true self, it's whenever they're ready to show you. I remember Trish asking me "is he or is he not the one," I guess not. After a month of being in jail I found out I was pregnant, we had a son I named him Eric.

No Chaser

Straight Like That

I liked everything in life just how I liked my drinks straight no chaser. I've always been the type of bitch that just didn't give a shit, didn't give one care of what people thought. How I dressed, wore my hair, talked, walked it was all to benefit me, now not to brag but I looked good doing it. My life was pretty simple don't fuck with me and I won't fuck with you. My only problem was I was addicted to sex, well maybe not addicted, but when I wanted it I had to have it.

I enjoyed dating, but it wasn't my priority. Men were like pennies to me you could find them just about anywhere. I was currently dating a guy named Mike I met a few months ago at one of my girl's birthday parties. I had to use the bathroom and when I opened the door there he was fucking some chick. I had got a chance to see his dick, and lets just say dude was working with a platinum package, so you already know I wanted to see what it was about for myself.

We talked for about a week before we went on our first date, of course I told him the real reason why I wanted to talk to him, he laughed, but after that first date he found me to be so serious. I had on a dress that day, and no panties. After dinner I fucked him in the car in the restaurant parking lot. I told him I wanted to see if it was worth making plans for a second date. He looked at me like I was crazy, but hey he's still hanging around, guess I didn't sound too crazy.

I have to say his dick is the bomb, but that hasn't stopped me from looking and talking to other men, hell I'm single, and dating doesn't qualify as being in a relationship. I mean some people date to find their soul mate, and some people do it for sport. I'm somewhere in between there.

It was a Friday night, and I had a date with Michael, Michael was not Mike. I just had two men with similar names. Michael was someone I had known for five years; now Michael was one of those people in search for their soul mate. He still had hopes that it could be me, and I still gave him hope that it could be. It was something about him I just couldn't shake off. The only problem was he had a dumb ass baby mama.

He was an example of the reason why I never wanted to date men with children, because if the child mother still had feelings, you best believe you were going to have some problems. It was about five months into us dating, and I was over his house. We had just starting fucking when there was a knock at the door; it was crazy baby mama.

I was like fuck her and told him to keep fucking me, thinking eventually the bitch would leave. I look up and this bitch standing at the bedroom door! He said he had taken back his key but apparently she made a copy. Now I ain't a scared bitch and she didn't have any weapons so I was cool. Michael had put his underwear on so he could try and get her out the house, but I couldn't help but to notice that all while she's asking how could he do this to her she's staring at my pussy. So I asked her "would you like to fuck me too?" Lets just say I had a way with words, and I let her and Michael fuck me that night.

I think Michael fell more in love with me that night, and unfortunately I think his baby mama did too. She thought that we were now cool, and that she should be included in everything that him and I did, so I gave them both a break, an entire year. When we finally started back dating, baby mama was in a new relationship, but thought that now her and her dude should be included in Michael and I sex time. I told the bitch she was crazy, just a fuck and that she needs to get her mind right, she's back to hating me now...lol.

Michael and I went to one of his cousins' social club parties. I loved their parties. You were guaranteed to have a wild and freaky night. I always left there horny, and tonight wasn't any different. When we made it to Michael's truck, he stood at the back door nodding his head towards the window. I knew that meant he was asking could we have sex. You already know I was down.

I would always wear dresses when we went out; it made for easier excess especially when out in public. Michael was already in the backseat with dick in hand. I lifted my dress, and sat this hot pussy right on his thick hard dick. Damn he had some good dick, and I sure didn't mind riding it. After we both climaxed I told him we needed to hurry home so we could continue. I wasn't going to let the car be the only time we fucked tonight.

We went back to my place, and headed straight to the bedroom. I reached over into my nightstand and grabbed one of my bullets, I gave it to him and gestured towards my pussy and told him to play with it.

For some reason it always felt better when someone else used my toys on me. I could feel my sheets getting soaked beneath me. I really loved foreplay; with the right person it was the fucking best.

Michael was finish with the bullet, and told me to turnover so he could hit it from behind, that was another favorite position of mine. What started as slow strokes quickly got faster, and my body cried out in enjoyment. I mean I really had tears coming from my eyes, that's how good it was. It was always good with him, you would think I'd make the decision to be his soul mate, but it just wasn't in me at the moment. Hell I was still young, and still wanted to do whatever the fuck I pleased.

I laid there in bed not making a move, my body was worn out, and I think his was too. We looked at each other and just smiled before falling asleep, out of all the guys he was the only one I let stay at my house longer than twenty-four hours. It was four in the morning, and I thought I heard someone outside. I got up to take a peek out the window; it was Mike getting into his car. I wondered what could he have wanted.

It was noon and Michael was leaving to go home. I told him I would call him later. I decided to call Mike to see why he was at my house this morning, but he did not answer. Now I was even more concerned because he always answered my calls. I hoped that maybe he was just too busy and would call me back. It was a Saturday chill day at home for me laundry, cleaning, and relaxing.

It was eight o'clock at night and I still haven't heard from Mike. I was just about to call him again when my phone rang. "Hey Mike, I answered." He explained to me that he was busy at work earlier that's why he didn't answer my call. I asked him was he coming over, he said he'd be over in about an hour; I thought I'd ask him when he gets here about this morning.

It was a little after nine when there was a knock at the door, I figured it must be Mike and it was. I opened the door to let him in, but little did I know Michael was standing outside with him. "What the hell is going on," I asked. Apparently this morning Mike was doing a drive-by...go figure. The reason I saw him getting back into his car is because he got out to check and see if that was Michael's truck in my driveway. Mike and Michael are fucking best friends. Now I know why Mike face looked familiar when I met him, apparently for the second time. I met him five years ago when I met Michael, but Mike had moved to Florida right after, so I never got a chance to get to know him.

Here we were standing in my living room, and I'm thinking it's not like I'm committed to either one of them. I do know I had showered and had a clean pussy waiting for Mike's dick, and like I said when I wanted it I had to have it. We all sat and talked for a minute trying to get some understanding of the situation, but the only understanding I wanted was am I fucking both or one of them tonight, so I asked. Like I said before I had a way with words.

Two platinum dicks in my bed at the same time, how fucking amazing! They took turns between my pussy and my mouth. I let them have their way with me. I truly enjoyed the both of them. Michael had to leave for work, so that left Mike and I to finish alone. I sexed them every week sometimes with one sometimes with both, but it was all good, straight like that.

A True Love Letter

My Dear Terrell

My Dear Terrell,

It's only been seven months since you went away. I've been like an introvert up until now, writing seems to be the only way I can express how I am feeling. It's been inconceivable who would've thought you would leave me this way. I think about you every day, how as teenagers all the fun and laughter we shared. How we talked about our future plans after high school, and the day that we fell passionately in love. From that day you remained my one and only true companion. Through all the bullshit I never left your side. I remember when we found out we were going to have a child how excited you were. By the way she's gotten a little bigger, and when she frowns she looks just like you. Then I remember that bitch around the corner that said she was pregnant with your child, and you thought it could be because you had slept with her, I was stressed about it but continued to be with you. Remember we had plans to get married on my twenty-first birthday, well tomorrow's the day. You were always there to protect me, never insensitive but always influential. I miss your exotic walk, extraordinary tastes, your embrace, your total affection. God knows this has been so excruciating for me, but I can't question him why, but inside I've been wanted to die. I'll dig this letter in the dirt maybe it'll find its way to you. I know I'll never find another like you. I'll always love you my Dear Terrell.

Even if they weren't my Stories

They were someone's

Tales Of Love And Life

It's been said that love is something that shouldn't be rushed. That it comes in time you just have to have patience, but no one ever said what to do when you finally find that special someone to love. No one ever said it because no one really knows.

It's been said that love comes and love goes and where your heart will end up nobody knows. The question has been asked do people really care, and the question has been answered some do some don't.

Those

Spoken Words

Dear God
So many things in my Life that I wish I could change
I know as I write these words that my Life will never be the same
A once pure soul now lives corrupt in this world so much sin
I don't know where to begin

LIFE

The rain is coming down seems like my pain never ending

Looking out the window with pillow cuffed beneath me

thinking life has better things in store for me

Lonely days and lonely nights hungry for something different

to feel my appetite

Same old job punching the clock wondering when will my

watch stop tick tock

Watching the news this TV blues trying to feel their havoc, but it's

something you can't endure unless it happens to you then life's not

laughable anymore

Hustling in the streets cause some path in your life you didn't

complete

Now you struggle every day to make ends meet

Never time to sleep

Dancing for cash a few nights selling ass

Not to knock your hustle but what's left when your body is decrepit

Trying not let my animosity take over my heart for things in my life

that I wish I could change or never had taken part

Dealing with the cards we were dealt but did you ever stop

to think who's behind the shuffle

So much chaos you took her life then yours

Knowing she had babies to raise another child lost then

we preach what about our children

Why?

When we're taking their lives too

So entangled in life wicked ways like a fly caught in a web

The only way out is death

But does it have to be

So much compassion you love me and I love you

Now someone's threating me

You could've told me I wasn't the only one

Which I would like to be to that fearless one

That won't further mislead me down this road of destruction

I must be reborn

Life is truly a dream fantasy part of your imagination

both expressions of your mind

Together being whatever you make it

Life

REBORN

From birth a soul so pure embraced with what should be

real love for the first time

No clear vision of what's ahead of you

Pain of the world unknown to you

To laugh and be joyous is what you want to do

Spirit still live and blessed for it has not yet been put

to these worldly tests

To be nurtured is a comfort zone

But now you're grown and left to be alone

Disaster strikes you unknowingly

Disease inflict your body uncontrollably

Wicked ways of men and self burden you

Instead of praying you seek other hideous things

To entertain you

Life not right and you wonder why

Now you break down and cry

No more mommy singing lullabies

For your selfish and evil ways weren't taught to you and if

by chance they were it's your mind

So that's what you chose to do

Prayer turns into sin for you never had faith to begin

Slowly drowning knowing you can't swim

Hoping that a lifeguard jump in to help you breath again

But what if it's too late and death swallows you

Now your chance for new life has come to an end

Now you wish you could pray again

No chance to be Reborn

Black Men

Hey how are you my black men

Just wondering if you had some time to spend

I know as black women you don't think we appreciate our

black men but I'm here to tell you I clearly understand

We walk around admiring you trying to get enough ambition

to talk to you hoping that you notice us too

So we flaunt our ass all this just to get next to you

We look at you from head to toe

Trying to figure out what we think we know

Damn that nigga riding in Benz

He must have money to blow

So now you're seeing our essence

And it's feeling real good

We've got together now the real shit begins

To make it short all that exterior we saw

When we met you is now coming to an end

But we never allowed ourselves to see the interior

Of our beautiful black men

Now we start to tear him apart and show animosity

when he choose to have a change of heart

I love my black men never any other color

Cause my black men are some real cool brothers

Even when you go astray I don't turn my head the other way

To each is own and that's what you chose

But you're still my black men even if one or two

black women did you wrong

Then we have babies sure it takes two to tangle but we chose to have

them even when he said he wasn't ready to take part

And then get mad cause he can't do what's not in his heart

Call the cops on him talk bad about him

But didn't he tell you he didn't love you from the start

We bridge carding it

FIA cashing it

Then look down on our black when he's going

Through his struggle like he ain't shit

When the damn government paying for half our shit

now ain't that a bitch

Half of us walk around looking like we got a college degree

When all we have is a GED

It seems we've forgotten behind every strong black man

Has to be a strong black woman

But we're too concerned about what we're getting

I'm sorry some of us don't understand

I'm sorry some don't appreciate you

But you dazzle me

You amaze me

Your diversity

Your essence

When you're exquisite it's evident

From the thunder and power in your voice

You are truly my black men

I love you

M.I.T.F.D

I know I was conceived by what you thought was real love

My little life is just beginning

I know you don't feel me yet but I feel that I cause you a threat

I know you're falling out of love with your guy

You may feel you've been deceived

And even though I'm a little seed

I still know mommy's cry

Wipe your tears away mommy it'll be okay

For little me will be on the way

What's that I hear you don't want me

You and daddy are falling apart

I thought I was your beloved

So what do I have to do with that part

Please mommy that would be a blunder

Didn't God put me here

That's what an angel said in my undeveloped ear

Keep your composure your acting irrational

For my life is just as precious

As your mother thought yours

Feel that pain in your stomach

That's my God helping me to cry

Trying to let you know mommy

I don't want to die

Please take this into consideration

If you don't want to watch me grow

Just give me to another mommy

That would love to see me put on a show

It's been twelve weeks and I notice that you cry almost every day

Why?

I assume that you're keeping me by now

Mommy I never wanted to cause you pain

I thought babies were bundles of joy

You're started to cry heavier than before

What's that?

Something's coming in here!

It's not time yet!

What's that loud noise!

Mommy No!

Stop It Mommy!

Please Stop It!

It's hurting me and pulling me out of here!

All the times I listened to mommy

She never once heard my cry

I still love you mommy

Even though this has been

Murder In The First Degree.

Understanding & Confusing

Love

I fought for it with every uttered word from my tongue

And breathe from my body

Every sleepless night with eyes shut tight

With a wounded and misguided heart

I fought for it

With every word written that turned into a

Five-line sentence

I fought for it

Even with the thoughts of being deceived

And days when it became difficult to breath

I fought for it

Sacrificed my mind for my heart

Almost leaving me brain dead

Cause I was fighting for it

With beliefs that were no longer mine

I fought for it

Even as I write and speak these words

I still fight for it

Now you may think this is called

I fought for it

It's not

Its called Love

I fought for it

But it denied me.

Do I

Do I go against everything I ever loved

Do I go against his smile, his eyes, his nostrils that intrigue me

His laugh that fulfills me, and his touch that warms me

Do I go against not feeling like I'm getting all I deserve

Do I go against the meaningless conversations

The heartache of loving and not feeling the same in return

The I love you that are never reciprocated

The repeated I miss you but yet

I'm still alone

Do I go against my heart and everything I thought

and think we still can be

Do I go against the good and bad

Do I go against all these things for new love

Do I?

Beautiful

From the first time that I saw you

Not having a clue of who you were

There was something I saw in you that was

Beautiful

When I met you it was true

Then I fell for you I knew

Damn this is

Beautiful

You were so assertive

You were bonafide

You were my beloved

You were

Beautiful

To have lost you in such short time

Left me to wonder was this a lesson in time

I can still hear the clarity when you speak

Though our hearts been broken

Paths unchosen

But souls still frozen in that place in our mind

Where love is pure and we are still together

And you are still

Beautiful

Deeply

She told him she loved him deeply

But in the back of her mind she wondered

If he really knew what that meant

She thought In case he didn't know

She would clarify

I love you deeply mean that I have reached

Down to the depth of me

You know so deep where some people

Are afraid to reach

You know like when a diver

Dives into the ocean

But realize it's just too deep

I love you deeply mean my every day thoughts

Are consumed with you

Like when you tell me you are unhappy

I constantly think what more can I do

I love you deeply mean I just don't think of me

But more of you

I love you deeply means that I'll fight

For whatever you're fighting for

Your pain I won't ignore

I love you deeply means I couldn't imagine

my future without you

It means I'll ride this life

To the depths

With you.

Lifeline

Its connection is well needed

Without it is fatal

It is strong

It is what gives me life

Few things can make it weak and you are one

You are the ventricle that pumps life into my body and without you I

will surely die

You are my Heartbeat.

IF

Sometimes I wonder IF

You could live without me

Sometimes I wonder IF

It ever crossed your mind

Sometimes I wonder IF

We did things different where would we be

Would you still be here holding on to me

IF I told you the emptiness I feel

When we are apart

I wonder IF you would take time

To fulfill my empty heart

I wonder IF I fall

Would you be here to catch me

Opening up your heart to me

And never letting go

Sometimes I wonder how deep

This love can go

So IF I told you today

I'm never going away

I wonder IF you would do your best

To push me away

Or would you reach within me

And want me to stay

Surely the day will come

When I no longer have to wonder

IF

Deeply II

Damn I don't think you realize how deep

This rabbit hole go

I mean I know I told you I love you deeply

Like Monica I got love all over me

But can you really see

Stress on my heart when you're not next to me

Like I know God created me

But do you know you're the life of me

Like life's not right unless your heart beat for me

Like taking my last breath

But I don't want you to realize in my death

You're the one for me

So let your heart beat for me

And consume me with love eternally

And I promise I'll give you the best of me

I'll follow and let you take the lead role

You know God, us, then the kids

I hope you love me more than me

So we can walk this path equally

Make sense to me

The heart in the package reads handle with care

So please treat it gently.

Illusions

Good morning with an I love you

As he massaged my back

Worked his way down and massaged my feet

Minutes later he's out of sight

And the flow of water I hear

The aroma of apple cinnamon feels the air

Then his presents is felt

As my night gown slides off my body

And hands scoop beneath me

Carrying me off to a hot bath

Expressive is he

I know he loves me

As the touch of warm water soothes my back

Now out of sight again

Until he returns with breakfast in hand

Now I'm being fed while my body relaxes

Out of the water now I lay wet and naked in bed

Body oils cover me

Now I'm being caressed over and over again

He's so extraordinary

I'm fascinated once more as his body covers me

And part of him internally feels me

Hours pass

Irresistible is he as he cuffs and embraces

My body under his

Eyes begin to close and we lay asleep

Illusions of love and what could be

Now escapes me

These Illusions I see

That a perfect man lay next to me.

After sex

After sex when he cuddles me

I wonder what he's thinking

Holding my naked body and pulling me closer to him

Does it mean he loves me or was the sex so good

He just wants to hold me

I wonder what he's thinking

When my back is to his chest

My ass to his middle

And his one leg is wrapped around mine

Is he thinking this is her

Oh how I wonder

Positions now change and my body now embraces his

I know what I'm thinking

As my nose is close to his body and I inhale

As I rub my fingers over his head

I'm thinking this is him

The one I love

The one I'm in love with

The one I never thought I'd be laying next to

The one that makes me feel secure

Like I can do anything in this world

The one who inspires me

The one I choose to give my life to

The one I never want to lose

Damn after sex

When your bodies entwine

and souls exchange.

Him

I know it may seem illogical how one can come in such little time

and have great intent on ones heart

His intellect is what had me from the start and although it was that

man's mind that had me all entwined

It was his touch and dedication that proved so much

Fluent when he speaks and aspirations for the world made me

appreciate him even more

How could one ignore such greatness and love in

ones Soul.

Situation

When you find a place and space of your own

I know in my heart you'll be gone

Though this feeling of being comfortable

Is why you stay

I sometimes wonder

Do you love me anyway

I know when we make love

I feel connected to you in so many ways

Is it just sex for you or do you feel the same

There's no one to blame but me

For letting this situation happen so suddenly

I sometimes go in with closed eyes

For fear of what I don't want to see

When I love I give my all

That comes with having a

Passionate beautiful heart

Maybe that's why it always get torn apart

Is it that we're scared to experience something new

something that could actually be true

I know you won't be here long

In my heart you're already gone

Situation is crazy

I dream of one day having your baby

Not to be baby mama but wife the right life

Situation so many people involved

That would love to see us fall

Do we let them stop our success

Or do we continue to thrive

For that ambition to be the best

Situation at night when I lay next to you

And watch you sleep you give me a feeling

That only my body can speak

When I caress your head and kiss your cheek

I think is my present my future

Damn I get so scared

Situation I want to hold you everyday

Tell you how much I love you

Follow you around the house

But it's that fear that you'll turn me away

Situation there's not a day or night

When you're out of sight that I don't worry about you

thinking I wish you were here

I know you won't be here long

In my heart you're already gone

When you're ready to leave

I'll let you go

Situation is I'll still love you.

Last Love

I'm really missing you

Can't help to think you don't realize how much

I appreciated you

I'm in disbelief can't believe you abandoned me

leaves me to wonder did you really

Love me

Cause you did it so suddenly

I acknowledge I had my faults

But never once did I feel this in my heart

My body gets so shivery not having you to hold

Your space in bed remains

I sometimes at night imagine you there

But when I wake its very clear no one was ever there

This is injustice to me

We never really tried to intensify

Something that was deep within us

Love

We were both too head strong

I can't help but to worry about you

I pray that you're safe in all you do

I'm trying my best to endure this

Because your love and affection

Has become elusive and causing distress

I'll just take this as another one of God's test

Pain is love and life not always sweetlife

Right

My body is tired and heart decrepit

Maybe one day you'll find your way back

To complete me

Hope it be soon

Until then you will remain last love.

Heartache

And The

Storm

It came from deep within

Pain inflicted me as it made its way

Up through my body

Never once did I want to feel this way again

But it happened

Starting the same as always

When I put my love in another mans

Hands

I always enjoyed the silence

But not too much

Because that would mean I was

Permanently alone

Maybe it was how you wanted to see me

In the new shoes you bought

Or how my butt sits up with no butt shots

In the jeans you bought

Maybe it was the thickness of my lips

With my elusive hips

Or Maybe it was...you know what

Fuck Maybe!

Was it ever just the thought of loving me

Knowing the woman I am and can be

That the woman you see is the her for you

That my heart never gave up on you

That I'd love you for eternity

However long that may be

Have you ever once searched

The pureness and delicacies of my soul

Cause one can only fathom how a few rainy days

turns to darkness, bloodshot tears And fears of losing you

The only man that's not of my blood that I'd die for

not like taking my life but die while fighting for yours

At a ripe age and my heart still hitting pavement

Like my first crush only back then

I didn't know it was just lust

Trying to hold on to this heart

Before it gets completely bruised and bust

And I slowly drown in a sea of my own tears cause

I trusted this to be true or Maybe

Yes I went back to Maybe

Maybe you never experienced a love like mine

Cause your heart is blind and it's hard to find

Your destiny within me

But I guarantee that true love never deceives

For those words your words are forever tatted on me

Maybe if you took the time.

* * * *

It sucks to tell your man you love him

And he never says it back

You get an awe thank you

It sucks that you're in a relationship

That holds no meaningful conversations

Although it could but you know the other person

Is not going to reciprocate

It's like okay we're not about to do another year of this

I started to feel like if I was really "Her"

I wouldn't have to question it

That it would be so much more

Asked you about being a family

Still nothing has happened

So how am I to believe it ever will

* * * *

God knows I love you but I'm scared of a repeat

I'm scared that nothing is going to change

Scared that it'll seem good for a moment

Then right back to the same old thing

Words with action is good and I needed your words

I wanted to hear from your mouth

That you needed me

That you loved me

That you wanted us

I wanted your heart to beat the same as mine

Sad thing is I can't shake you even if I tried

* * * *

I tried so much to live for you and by that I mean

whatever you asked of me I did

Denying me

But that's how much I loved you

But then it was like okay what are we doing here

I would literally have to stop listening to music

To not think about you

* * * *

It's crazy that all I asked was for some communication

and what my future held with you

and I couldn't get that

After so many years I'm still not worth that

I never asked for much but yet the littlest thing

Was so hard to do

Hence the reason why I didn't believe

When you said you were scared of losing me

If the thought of losing me didn't make your heart

Do triple beats and sickness in your belly

You're definitely not scared

But with all that I won't deny that I

Miss you

I went to sleep with the phone in my hand

Hoping that he would text back

And praying that he would call

I want to stop loving you

But I don't know how

Truth is

I probably never will

I think you know how much I love you

So you think I'm not going anywhere

But hell I could leave work and die on the way home

(hope not) you get the point

Our days are not that long

I'm ready to start a life with the man

that wants what I want

That's not afraid to love me

Not scared of having a family other then his own

Who wouldn't mind calling me his wife

Who's willing to teach me things I don't know

We learn from each other

Who's ready to see me every day

Who can't go a day without checking

On me to make sure I'm okay

Who's willing to share not just the good moments

But the bad ones too

Who's busy as hell but still finds time

Who's scared of going through the rest

of their life without me

So they hear everything I'm saying

And make it a priority

Funny cause in my mind

I thought it was

You

You asked how could I consider him my man

When I don't know all there is to know about him

After all these years and I couldn't even tell you his favorite color

It's also funny when I tell the story of how I never met his

Mother

* * * *

At times I don't know what I am doing

I think I'm waiting for you to come save me

When I probably should be saving myself

I'm waiting on you to show me that things will be different

I think it but for some reason I'm not feeling it

I want to believe that it is you

But I find myself searching for the "her"

That once believed that to be true

Can you come and save me from this torment

That I'm putting myself through

Do you think that's something you can do

Although part of me died there's still a part

That's alive with hopes for you

But that's the part that can't swim

The part that's slowly drowning

Cause it keeps going further to the deep end

Do you think you can come save me

Before I completely die

Making this our final and last goodbye

I can't swim I'm slowly drowning

I'm reaching out but I can't find anything to hold on to

Help!!

Our should we just let this love die

* * * *

I am not Her

I am not her cause one would never confuse

Great sex over my intellect

One would never try to confound me into thinking

I mean more to them than what I really am

One would never take my virtues as a woman

And try to make me sin for them

Bringing out the darkness within

Trying to make me a culprit of a crime

I have yet to begin

When the only crime I am guilty of

Is loving a man

If you don't see the longevity

Stop thinking you have to pacify me

in fear of completely breaking me

Cause if I'm really your world

You would breath for me

There would be no other woman you see

I tried to be optimist for you

Relinquished my former life for you

But I can't make a blind man see

Unfortunately that's not part of my creativity

If I am wrong then right me

But I'll know for sure when you wake

And find it difficult to breath

Without me

Her happiness was slowly fading

Internally she was slowly dying

Outside she glowed with a smile

No one would ever know her pain

Unless she told them

This made her a woman of many faces

But internally she would remain

Faceless

What I wanted to say was FUCK YOU! What the fuck you know about love anyway? Do you think it's a fucking game that I'm out here to play...FUCK YOU!

I wish I never knew you

I wish you never came into my life

I wish you never allowed me to give you my all

FUCK YOU! AND FUCK ME! For allowing myself to...what the fuck you know about love when you never had real love anyway...FUCK YOU! FUCK YOU! FUCK YOU! That's what I wanted to say but my LOVE WAS SO DEEP IT DIDN'T ALLOW ME TO

It all came to a crashing end

Life saved by the airbag ejected

As much as I wanted to I decided not to cry

From the pain within

Thinking you will not win

So instead I put on my grown woman clothes

Game face too

And stepped back into the world like the strong woman

I have always been

In the middle of the storm there was peace and clarity

I never heard things more clearly as I did then

A New
Love Is Calling

At that moment he was like a breath of fresh air

And I was enjoying it so I kept

Breathing

My God is this him has my want and need come to an end

Can I finally let go of what I told my own self to be true

Should I believe that all things happen for a reason

In all the pain that I endured

Thanks for not allowing it to weaken me

Thanks for not allowing me to be coldhearted

I asked for signs to see

I prayed and hope he prayed he's the one for me

****

He came at a time when I was broken

heart swollen and life not looking to promising

I was starting to feel lifeless

But weeks of pain turned into days of pleasure

Feelings that I thought no other could give

He did

I allowed myself to be open to him

Soon to be submissive

And found myself drowning in him

Being covered with what felt like love

His smile captivates me

His touch weakens me

His mind empowers me

And I am completely fond of him

He has imposed on my heart

Now I forever want him

****

He amazes me with his creativity

His intellect is like having passionate sex

It pleases me

So entwine with his mind that when I close my eyes

I become him

Connected to his heart cause that's my favorite part

So I beat for him

Now that's some deep shit that some will never get

* * * *

With all the chaos

She lay quietly and patiently waiting

Praying that once the storm is over

He will see things SEE HER a little clearer

That even in her own storm

She NEVER

Rained on his

She prayed that once things settled

and the noise went away

He could finally HEAR HER

He could finally embrace her and taste her essence

He would finally see why he loved her

And not from a phone conversation

But because he could now take the time

to completely get to know HER.

****

He was how she didn't like her coffee

Strong and straight

But he wasn't coffee

He was her delicacy

He was like the morning water

that touches your face

And

The mint that touches your lips

Before entering your mouth

REFRESHING

At times he was like reading a book

A MYSTERY

He was her favorite cup of tea

TASTEFUL

He was her morning and night

Her sun, moon, and her stars

He was her world

And she was destined

To give him LIFE

* * * *

As she opened her eyes

She rolled to her side with phone in hand

She gazed at his picture in amazement

She always woke with him on her mind

He was her breath of air that she enjoyed breathing

Still gazing at his picture

She thought what wonderful characteristics of a man

She looked to the ceiling reaching to the heavens

And thanked God for such a beautiful creation

He was a man like no other

And God blessed her to be his

Or maybe she was his blessing

Either way she was in love

Unconditionally and Eternity

She would love him

In this life and in death

She would be his angel

* * * *

I wish I was a virgin meeting you for the first time

and it was you that took my virginity

Making me a woman that would birth babies

only for you

Because the love you give is amazing

Not just physically but mentally too

You are a man unlike no other

So the best I can do

is

devote my life to you

I found myself burying my face in the shirt
He left behind
His scent calmed me
And I slowly drifted to that other place
Imagining Him holding me

With All Her Imperfections

He Still Loves Her

What was beautifully created

Should never end

THANKS FOR

READING

In memory of my nephew

A Poem For Daniel

I was waiting on you
The Doctors had me dressed in blue scrubs
And
I couldn't wait to hold you in my arms
And Love You
But
When you came out the womb
You were fighting
To hold on
And I was fighting to stay strong
You were such a beautiful baby
A chubby one too
Your big cousin/brother
Couldn't wait for you to
Grow big so he could
Play with you
The entire family
Was waiting to love you
I had an entire life mapped out for you
And I know your parents did too
But God saw a better life for you
So now you're an angel in the heavens
Watching everything we do
So keep smiling down on us baby Daniel
But most of all keep smiling down on your
Mommy too
Love your Aunt that will always and forever
Think the world of you!

To My Readers

'

Thanks for taking the time to read my book; it means the world to me to finally be able to say I am an author. I wrote this book to show who I am as a writer and as a poet. Even when I was told that "no one wants to hear poetry, you are not Maya Angelou." Well I know I'm not and never tried to be, I enjoy just being me, but I do know there are many people out there like me that loves this genre of reading. My mind is like a blank piece of paper, ready to write whatever comes to mind. I wish I would've put more of an effort into my passion at a younger age, but it's never too late to do what you love. Those that know me know that Lola has been my alter ego for years; she gets me when the world does not. I am at the beginning of my journey, and I hope you will take this ride with me. I hope you enjoyed reading my book as much as I loved writing it, and keep a watchful eye for my second book...

NASTY

A

Novel

By

Lola London

KEN (KENNETH)

Kenneth is my name, but everybody always called me Ken, I heard that more than my government, I told my mom that should've been my name. Growing up my mom was a single parent trying to raise two badass boys. I was eleven, and my brother was fourteen when my father passed away. My father was some low life wannabe street nigga, who got his ass killed trying to do a drug deal. At least that's what my mom said when me, and my brother would piss her off. I had an uncle named Mike, my mom's younger bother who would help out with us sometimes, "so we won't end up like him," she would say referring to my father. Mike was like having the dad we never really had. It almost killed my mother when he passed away.

We moved to Detroit shortly after my mom's birthday, it would be the last birthday she would ever spend with her brother, two weeks after moving here he was murdered. Unfortunately my brother who was seventeen at the time was with him, and believed to have been murdered too. I say believed to because their bodies were never found, but hell what else would it be, what would make your loved ones not return to you other than death. I wanted to move back home, after only two weeks of living in this shitty city two people that mattered to me the most gone, just like that, but it was no going back...